I0797840

the little book of Intuition

Wonderful things can happen to you too, when you start using the magic power of your subconscious mind.

the little book of Intuition

Simple practices for working with your sixth sense

THERESA CHEUNG

GODSFIELD

First published in Great Britain in 2025
by Godsfield, an imprint of
Octopus Publishing Group Ltd
Carmelite House
50 Victoria Embankment
London EC4Y 0DZ
www.octopusbooks.co.uk

An Hachette UK Company
www.hachette.co.uk

The authorized representative in the EEA
is Hachette Ireland,
8 Castlecourt Centre, Dublin 15,
D15 XTP3, Ireland (email: info@hbgi.ie)

Some of this material previously appeared
in *Working with Your Sixth Sense*

Distributed in the US by Hachette
Book Group
1290 Avenue of the Americas,
4th and 5th Floors
New York, NY 10104

Distributed in Canada by Canadian
Manda Group
664 Annette St., Toronto,
Ontario, Canada M6S 2C8

ISBN 978-1-84181-639-5

A CIP catalogue record for this book is
available from the British Library.

Printed and bound in China.

10 9 8 7 6 5 4 3 2 1

Publisher: Lucy Pessell
Designer: Isobel Platt
Senior Editor: Tim Leng
Assistant Editor: Samina Rahman
Production Controller: Allison Gonsalves
Illustrations: Bárbara Malagoli

Contents

Introduction

A sixth sense is not something that some people possess and others lack; some people are simply more aware of their abilities or more naturally sensitive than others. Rest assured that the potential is there within you; it is simply a forgotten art that needs to be rediscovered and developed.

Clues to Your Sixth Sense

- Have you ever had dreams that later seemed to come true?
- Have there been times in your life when you experienced déjà vu, or the feeling that you have been through something before?
- Have you experienced an inexplicable attraction to someone?
- Have you ever had a hunch that something would happen and then it did?

- Do you sometimes just know what someone else is thinking?
- Have you ever stared at someone, thinking they can't see you, only to find that they suddenly turn round and stare right back at you?
- Have you ever thought of someone and then found they telephoned a few minutes later?
- Do you sometimes sense the atmosphere in a room?
- Do you know when others are upset, angry or excited before they speak to you?
- Have you ever had a sudden feeling that you should, or should not, do something or be somewhere – then found out later that you should have listened to that feeling?

Even if you only answered "maybe" to just one of these questions, it is an indication that you have had what appears to be the simplest, most basic kind of psychic (sixth-sense) experience.

How to Use This Book

Consider this book your first step into a world of endless potential. By means of the techniques you will learn here you will strengthen your sixth sense, finding natural ways to tap into your wellspring of intuitive wisdom.

As you read the book you will be given practical and safe guidance on every aspect of your psychic development and how you can experience it in everyday life. You will be taken stage by stage through those hunches and vague thoughts that, when put together, make up your psychic potential – your silent power.

Psychic Exercises

The exercises throughout this book are not tests and there are no right or wrong answers. Just try them and see how you feel. It may take time for you to catch on, so maintain a positive attitude. Think of them as psychic workouts that flex your sixth-sense muscles. And, as with any physical workout, you will benefit from a cool-down afterwards: any simple act that brings you back to normal, such as grabbing a snack, going for a walk or chatting to a friend.

Some of the exercises ask you to visualize. If you struggle to form mental images, as a lot of us do, simply write down or describe to yourself – out loud or with your thoughts – what you want to visualize. It has the same transcendent effect.

What is Your Sixth Sense?

If you have ever had a feeling that something might happen and it did, or had a dream that came true, or thought something at exactly the same time someone else did, then you may be using your sixth sense without even realizing it.

The exercises in this chapter are designed to help you become more aware of the world of your sixth sense, intuition or psychic power. (In this book the terms intuition, sixth sense and psychic power are interchangeable.) Understanding the way you receive information from your sixth sense is a step towards building it, so in the pages that follow we look at three main areas of psychic ability: clairvoyance, clairaudience and clairsentience. As you read the descriptions and work through the exercises, see if any of your instincts draw you to any of these areas in particular.

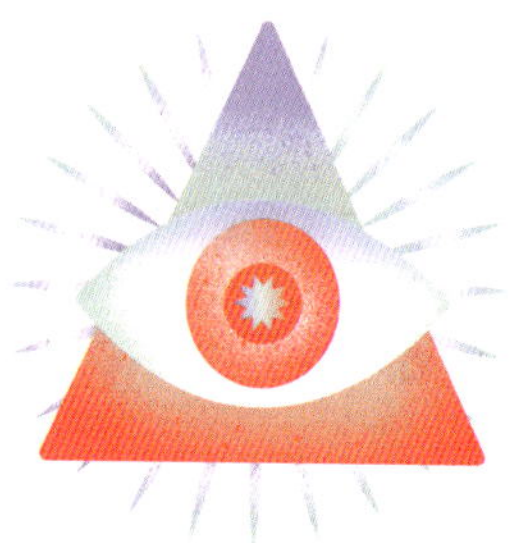

Connecting to Your Sixth Sense

All of us have a sixth sense. So, you may ask, why aren't more of us using it? Let's try to explain by giving an example. If someone lived in the dark for years, their eyes would adjust to the absence of light; over time that person would actually be able to see better in the dark than in the light. It's the same with our sixth sense. Once civilization and technology came along, people didn't have to rely as much on being super-alert to stay alive and keep away from danger, and they simply got lazy and stopped sensing things around them.

In other words, if you don't use your psychic ability, you lose it. You need to rediscover, train and develop it every day, in much the same way that you would build up your physical fitness. A fundamental principle of sixth sense is that personal responsibility makes you the one accountable for discovering and developing your sixth sense, and for where you take your life from here.

Developing your sixth sense is a journey of rediscovery and self-discovery: rediscovering your inborn psychic ability and discovering who you are and where you are going. Once you understand this, you can begin to move forward, using what you discover to make the most of your life in every way. So where you do you start? You start by crossing a very special line – the line between your non-psychic side (your physical self) and your psychic side (your thoughts).

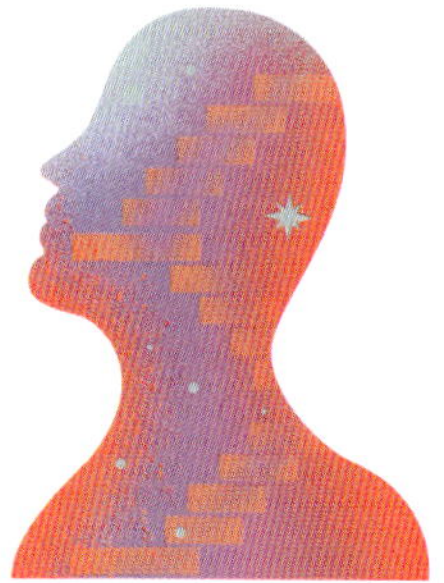

Psychic Workouts

The following exercises are designed to help you become more aware of the world inside your head and beyond your senses.

EXERCISE:

Growth and Decay

By paying attention to natural objects, this exercise encourages you to focus on the universal lifecycle. The more you do this, the more likely it is that you will begin to feel as if you are a part of an energy force passing through and around you.

1. Focus on a natural object, such as flowers growing in a pot or leaves falling from the trees.
2. Once you have got used to the feelings and shapes of growth and decay, try to tune into them even when you don't have an object in front of you to inspire that vision. This is a completely new way of looking at things, so give yourself plenty of time. The idea is that growth and decay aren't just words or objects; they are living forces that evoke images or associations in your mind. This is the start of psychic vision.
3. You are now ready to move on to other themes, such as the world of colour; what feelings or images do they inspire in you? Or you could contrast the feelings inspired by living things, such as animals or plants, with those provoked by inanimate things such as rocks or crystals.

EXERCISE:
Different Levels

This is a simple thinking exercise that you can do at any time, anywhere. Choose something familiar that you see every day – your coat, for example. Now you are going to think about it on four different levels.

1. Just think about the coat itself. What colour is it? Where did you buy it? What good or bad times have you had while wearing it?
2. Think of coats in general – everywhere.
3. Think of the purpose of coats: why do people wear them?
4. Think about coats in the abstract sense. For instance, they can be a symbol of protection and warmth, so let your mind linger on images of fire or comforting soup.

EXERCISE:

Staring at a Plant

This exercise is not as simple as it sounds, so don't become discouraged if you don't get immediate results.

1. Observe a young plant closely, paying special attention to its colour, shape and texture. Let the following thought fill your mind: This plant will one day become a bigger plant.

2. Now picture in your mind this bigger plant – see what it will one day become.

3. In time you may begin to see a mist or cloud surrounding the plant, or an image in your mind of the plant in flower. It isn't the staring that produces this effect; it is your understanding that every living being is surrounded by energy and has a destiny in store for it. If you can't see anything yet, don't worry. Just thinking about this idea will help enormously with your psychic development.

Tuning In

Now it is time to learn more about how you can receive psychic information. There are many ways in which such information can come to you, and each and every person has a specific way that works best for them.

Don't worry if it isn't immediately clear to you which method of psychic awareness you are drawn to, or if you are drawn to more than one. For now, just keep observing yourself and thinking about the way you think. In time, things will fall naturally into place.

Don't try to force things, just keep the ideas of the last few pages firmly in the back of your mind. The more you feel sympathy in yourself with the ideas of respect and awe, the more your sixth sense will grow automatically without your worrying about it. The more you will realize that the most reliable place to look for guidance is your higher self.

Clairvoyance

Have you ever seen images in your head? Perhaps you saw yourself passing an exam before you heard that you had passed? Perhaps you visualized yellow flowers in your mind's eye and, when you went on a date, saw that each table at the restaurant had a vase with little yellow flowers? If you have had experiences similar to these, you might be receiving psychic information through clairvoyance.

Clairvoyance literally means "clear seeing". It is the power to see an event or an image in the past, present or future.

Do You Process Information Visually?

If you answer "yes" to any of the questions below, you may be a strongly visual person and therefore more likely to receive information through clairvoyance.

- Do you think in pictures?
- Do you notice what things look like, rather than how they sound, feel, taste or smell?
- Are you an art lover?
- Are you fascinated by the appearance of people, objects or the environment?

Subjective Clairvoyance

Many clairvoyants get their insights internally – through their mind's eye; this is called subjective clairvoyance. It can come in the form of lights, images, symbols, colours or dreams, but some clairvoyants describe the images they receive as being projected from their "third eye" (see page 94) – as if it were a television or movie screen just in front of their forehead.

We all have the ability to develop subjective clairvoyance. Many of the exercises in the next chapter (see pages 30–47) will help you develop your ability to think in pictures, and thus your clairvoyant potential to see the future in pictures. For now you might want to try the following exercise.

EXERCISE:
Colour Vision

This exercise is all about impressions, so try not to think too much about what you are doing.

1. Cut out a 13cm (5in) square piece of white paper.
2. Using a felt tip, draw a circle and colour it blue. Now colour around that circle in orange.
3. Look at this card for two minutes. Don't stare too intently; just keep your eyes focused on the card for as long as you can.
4. Now close your eyes. You will see a faint likeness of the card in your inner vision, although the colours might change. Watch this inner image until it fades. Make no attempt to alter it.
5. Try to do this every day for five days. After a while you should find that you see the card clearly in your mind whenever you wish. All you need to do is close your eyes and wait!
6. Keep doing this for another week. Then one day, when you see the card with your eyes closed, simply open your eyes. The image should not disappear, but will be hanging there suspended in space – a vision.

Clairaudience

Have you ever heard sounds or voices that you know are real, even though you know they aren't happening in the "real world"? Have you ever been convinced that you heard someone calling you, even when they weren't? Have you ever heard voices warning you not to do something, or telling you to do something? If you have had these or similar experiences, you may be receiving psychic impressions through clairaudience.

Clairaudience literally means "clear hearing" and is the ability to receive psychic impressions through sound.

Do You Process Information Aurally?

If you answer "yes" to any of the following questions, the chances are that you have a tendency towards clairaudience.

- Are you a good listener?
- Do you describe your experiences in terms of the sounds you hear or what you are listening to?
- Do you find that certain sounds and noises are just unbearable?
- Do you have a flair for words?
- When you meet someone or go to a particular place, does a familiar song or piece of music pop into your head?

EXERCISE:

Listen to Your Inner Ear

We all receive a constant stream of information from our intuition, and a certain amount is clairaudient. You just need to remember to listen.

1. Seat yourself in a quiet place, close your eyes and relax. Put your concentration on the right, lower side of your head, to a point in the region of your inner ear. Now simply wait.

2. Through practice you will be able to tell if the voices you hear come from your intuition or are merely your own daily thoughts. Listen carefully: your intuition speaks to you in a kind, loving and gentle way; self-talk tends to be a little harsher and more critical.

3. You may find that you have a particular psychic ear – meaning that either your left or right ear is the one in which you will hear psychic impressions.

Clairsentience

Clairsentience, often described as clear thinking or clear knowing, is the ability to receive intuitive insight or information through your senses of smell, touch and taste. Whether you know it or not, you have probably already received information in this way. For example, you may have sensed an atmosphere when you entered a room.

Do You Process Information Emotionally?

If you answer "yes" to any of the questions below, you probably have strong clairsentient tendencies.

- Are you empathetic or compassionate towards others?
- Are you often affected by the moods of people close to you?
- Do you get a bad taste in your mouth, butterflies in your stomach or a tight feeling in your chest when something doesn't feel right?
- Do you smell things for no reason, such as roses when you are feeling happy?
- Can you sense the atmosphere in a room before anyone has spoken to you?

Developing Your Potential

In the next two chapters you will find various exercises to help develop your clairsentient potential. These are the starting points for most people, but if you are not sure how your psychic ability manifests itself, try the exercise overleaf.

The Way Ahead

This chapter has introduced you to the three main areas of psychic ability: clairvoyance, clairaudience and clairsentience. Many of the exercises in this book are designed to develop one or more of these areas. You may find that you are drawn to all three methods, but as you read on you may also begin to notice that your instincts attract you to one method in particular.

EXERCISE:

Tuning Into a Day at the Beach

1. This exercise can help you get in touch with the way you receive psychic information.

2. Close your eyes and breathe deeply. Gently relax. In your mind's eye, imagine yourself on a sandy beach on a beautiful sunny day. You can smell the sea air; you can hear the seagulls. A warm, gentle breeze lifts your hair. You hear and see the waves gently lapping on the shore. You can feel the heat of the sun on your skin. Your feet are bare and you feel the sand between your toes. You bend down to touch the cool water. You walk along the beach, feeling calm, relaxed and happy. You see an ice-cream stand ahead and buy an ice-cold vanilla cone. You taste it in your mouth and feel the refreshing coolness slide down your throat.

3. Now open your eyes slowly and think about what you experienced. Which one of your senses was it easiest for you to get in touch with? Was it sight or visual images (clairvoyance)? Was it sound (clairaudience)? Or was it smell, touch and taste (clairsentience)?

Working With Your Subconscious

If you want to tap into your subconscious or creative powers, you need first to build your imagination. The subconscious mind doesn't know the difference between reality and fantasy or imagination. Ideas that are formed in your mind are real, and everything that you tell the subconscious mind to be the truth is the truth. Second, you need to learn to control your thoughts.

Psychics and mystics believe that through thought-control techniques, such as relaxation, concentration and meditation, you can tap into your subconscious mind and thereby influence the events that occur in your life. When you meditate, you set up powerful forces that emanate from yourself and influence the world around you.

Sacred Space

In the pages that follow you will learn how to build your imagination and your powers of concentration. But before you do that, you need to create a special place in which you can carry out your psychic-development work: your sacred space. This place will represent your sanctuary and your doorway to another dimension.

Having a place where you will not be interrupted is the most important part of your sacred space. It doesn't need to be large: it can be the corner of a room, or simply a portable box with a candle and a special cloth that you carry around with you. It can be located anywhere, but it is up to you to make yours special to you.

Making Your Sacred Space

In a perfect world the guidelines given below would be easy to follow. In the real world they are sometimes hard to accomplish. Just do the best you can.

Do:

- Find a place where you won't be disturbed.
- Choose objects that are special to you.
- Use soft lights or candles.
- Surround yourself with comforting sounds – gentle music, sounds from nature or even just silence.

Don't:

- Clutter your space with unnecessary objects.
- Use bright lights – they can be distracting.
- Bring your mobile phone; turn it off when you enter your sacred space.

EXERCISE:

Progressive Relaxation

Relaxation is vital for working with your sixth sense. There are two good kinds of technique to learn – progressive relaxation and rhythmic breathing – and before you start any psychic exercise, you may want to begin with one of these two techniques.

Progressive relaxation is a wonderful way to begin your psychic work, because the more relaxed you are, the easier it is to get in touch with your psychic power.

1. Lie on the floor and make yourself comfortable. Take a deep breath and tense all your muscles.
2. As you breathe out, release the tension and send warm, soothing thoughts and energy to every part of your body, start at your feet and move up to the top of your head. You can do this by saying to yourself, "My feet are relaxed…my ankles are relaxed…my knees are relaxed", and onwards to the top of your head.

EXERCISE:
Rhythmic Breathing

You can use this method to relax at any time – before psychic work, after a long day or even if you can't get to sleep at night.

1. Begin rhythmic breathing from your stomach, breathing naturally, but slowly.
2. Slowly inhale through your nostrils for a count of five.
3. Hold for a count of five, and then exhale slowly for a count of five.
4. Imagine and feel warm energy flowing through your body. Feel the pause of peacefulness in between each breath.

Grounding

Every time you finish your psychic exercises you need to ground yourself and reconnect with the physical world, so that you can return to your daily life. Grounding can be different for everyone, so here are some examples of how you might do it:

- Try some stretches to reinvigorate yourself.
- Make a cup of tea.
- Eat a snack.
- Call a friend.
- Go for a walk or do some stretching.
- Write down your psychic experiences in a journal.

The Power of Imagination

When you imagine or visualize something, you see mental images, and these images have a meaning. Your job is to find out what these images are trying to tell you.

The exercises that follow will help you develop creative ways to use your imagination and strengthen your psychic powers. From now on, every time you do an exercise, try to set the mood by working in your sacred space (see pages 32–33) if you can, and by doing some relaxation exercises (see pages 34–35) before you work. And don't forget to ground yourself (see page 36) when you have finished.

EXERCISE:
Be Swept Away

This exercise will help to stimulate your imagination from the outside.

1. Find an illustrated book of fairy tales and spend some time just looking at the pictures. Think back to when you were a child and your parents read you a fairy tale. While you may remember hearing the story, what you probably remember most are the pictures and the feelings they provoked. Whether it was the sun setting or a fire-breathing dragon, the picture was real to you and you were absorbed by it. For a few moments you experienced it deeply in your imagination.
2. As you look at the pictures now with adult eyes, you may begin to notice feelings inside yourself that feel both familiar and new at the same time. This is a sign that the pictures are working their magic and that you are getting through to your psychic centre via your imagination.

EXERCISE:
From I to Y

This exercise will help to stimulate your imagination from the inside.

1. Draw a large I and a large Y close to each other on a piece of paper. Look at both letters, then cover up the Y shape with your hand and look only at the I. In your mind's eye, let the I transform itself into a Y. See the line dividing and turning outwards.
2. Try it again, only this time try to see one arm growing faster than the other.
3. Do it again and see one arm waiting for the other to complete before it moves. See in your mind's eye one of the arms moving and, when it stops, the other arm moving.

EXERCISE:

The Cross

At first you may think you can't see anything, but keep trying and you will succeed. With a bit of practice and patience, anyone can visualize.

1. Close your eyes and imagine a cross – any kind of cross that you like.
2. Hold this image in your mind and slowly rotate it until it is upside down.
3. Continue to rotate it until it has gone a full 360 degrees and is upright again.
4. When you have finished, leave your cross upright. You should always leave your visualization as you find it; if you don't, you might feel a bit unbalanced afterwards.

EXERCISE:
Visualize Everyday Objects

This exercise lays the foundation for psychic vision.

1. Practise closing your eyes and visualizing everyday objects, such as your watch, your keys, your mobile phone, and so on, in as much detail as possible.

EXERCISE:
People-Peeping

Use this exercise to hone your powers of imagination.

1. The next time you find yourself in a busy area where there are lots of people, find somewhere comfortable to sit and simply watch the passers-by going about their lives (don't stare, because this could alarm people).
2. Inevitably someone will catch your eye. As they walk by, keep their image in your mind and try to imagine where they are going or what their job is. Don't guess – try to visualize it. Pay attention to everything that you feel and imagine.

Concentration

Think of a time when you were so focused on what you were doing that you were able to block out all distractions. How can you re-create this level of concentration when doing your psychic exercises? If you don't think you can, try the exercise opposite and think again.

EXERCISE:

Walking Backwards

This exercise will improve your concentration and boost your psychic ability.

1. The evening is the best time to perform this exercise, so before you go to bed choose a quiet, comfortable place where you can pay attention to your thoughts and won't be interrupted.
2. Take a deep breath to relax your body and prepare your mind.
3. Start from this moment and remember the events of your day backwards until you reach the moment you got up.
4. If you get stuck, go back a bit and then work forward to untangle yourself. Your mind will have a tendency to wander, but don't force things or feel tense; simply shift your focus back to the task in hand. You may only manage five- or ten-second bursts, but this is enough to help you become more open to your psychic impressions.

EXERCISE:

Concentration Creation

This is such a powerful exercise to improve your concentration that you might want to practise it every day.

1. Make sure you aren't tired or hungry, then remove as many distractions as you can. Sit in a relaxed and upright position on the floor or in a chair that is comfortable, but not too comfortable.
2. Close your eyes and tell yourself firmly that you are "good" at concentrating. By repeating "I'm good at concentrating" you are programming your subconscious mind to believe that you have this skill. Repeat these words in whatever way suits you: write them, read them or say them over and over again.

3. Now give your mind a one-minute assignment. Tell it that you are going to write, read or say "I'm good at concentrating" for one whole minute. Set an alarm and do the one-minute assignment with all your attention. The first few times you try this your mind may start to wander. Don't get upset – just be patient and persist. Remember: you are the one who controls what goes on in your mind. If you become aware you are thinking about something else, stop, say "no" and return to your assignment with greater intensity.

4. When you are able to concentrate for one whole minute without being distracted, increase the period to two, three, four and then five minutes. Then make it harder for yourself. Introduce distractions: turn on the television, keep your eyes open, sit in a busy room. Repeat the exercise under these conditions until you are able to concentrate for five minutes.

5. This may take about three or four weeks to master, so don't worry if you don't get the hang of it right away. Once you are able to concentrate your mind, you can transfer these skills to your psychic development.

Meditation

The ultimate form of concentration is meditation. Meditation can help you receive intuitive guidance, because it relaxes your mind and makes you less easily distracted. Over time, a daily meditation of 10 minutes will work wonders for your psychic development.

If you feel uncomfortable with the term "meditation", try thinking of it as a time of stillness, quiet or even prayer. Try meditating at different times of the day to see which works best for you.

EXERCISE:
Fly Away

This simple exercise is a good starting point if you haven't meditated before.

1. Sit or lie down in your sacred space (see pages 32–33). Most people prefer to sit upright, but if you prefer lying down, that's fine. Make sure that your back is supported or straight, and that your body is open – don't cross your arms and legs; if you are physically open, you are more likely to be emotionally open.
2. Allow your eyes to close. Breathe in deeply, taking in a long, slow breath from your stomach, filling your lungs completely, gently holding the breath in for a moment and then releasing the air slowly. Focus on nothing but your breathing.
3. As you breathe, tell yourself that you are willing to develop your psychic potential. Let your fears, doubts and negative thoughts dissolve in a haze of golden light. If distracting thoughts enter your mind, imagine them turning into a beautiful bird or butterfly before flying away, leaving you calm, clear and still.
4. When you feel ready, slowly open your eyes, stretch and return to normal.

Working With People

Telepathy may be one of the most common forms of intuitive experience that people have. For example, you may recall receiving a letter from someone you were thinking about, or you may have a bought a present for someone when they were just about to buy that item for themselves. Incidents like this may have occurred many times, but you may simply have dismissed them as guesswork or coincidence.

In this chapter there are exercises to develop your ability to read minds and understand people better. You will also learn how to send and receive thoughts and how to read auras: the electromagnetic energies surrounding all living things, which contain our thoughts and feelings and which can be seen or sensed by psychics.

Handling Sensitivity

When you are empathetic, someone else's feelings, emotions and attitudes can affect you so strongly that they almost feel like your own. When you develop your psychic ability, outside impressions tend to register more strongly, and you are more likely to receive impressions of feelings and situations that are not your own.

How Sensitive Are You?

If you answer "yes" to any of the questions below, the chances are that you are a sensitive, empathetic person and need to protect yourself.

- Are you easily persuaded by others to do things you normally wouldn't do?
- Do your moods change as you go from one group to another?
- Do you feel drained after being with people?
- Do you need lots of time alone?
- Do you always seem to know what others are feeling?
- Are you a touchy-feely person?
- Do you have a tendency to take on other people's problems?

Cutting the Thread

If you are naturally empathetic and find it hard to disconnect from others, try visualizing a way to separate yourself from them. You might imagine that you are cutting a thread between you and the other person, or you could visualize going into a special room and closing the door. It may help to visualize a protective bubble around you that no one can enter. Call upon the part of yourself that knows how to detach itself when feelings you get from others or your environment become overwhelming.

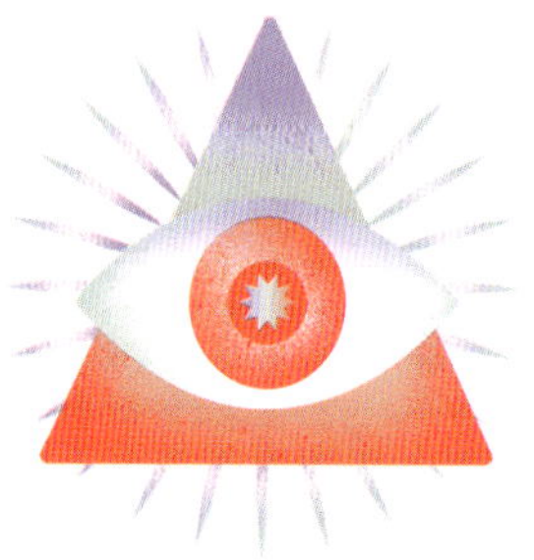

Auric Sight

Everything has a subtle energetic field, or aura, and the colours and forms of each aura are believed to be characteristic of the person, animal or thing they surround. These shift according to mood and state of health.

Seeing Auras

If you want to start seeing auras, you need first to feel as relaxed as possible. Breathe slowly and deeply for a few moments. Then, instead of looking directly at someone, look straight past them and glance casually in their direction, allowing your eyes to lose focus. The aim is to trick your rational mind by putting a lot of concentration on something else, keeping just a vague focus on the person whose aura you want to read.

Visions of auras tend to be lightning-quick, but the more you practise, the more natural it will feel and the more likely it is for the colour to become noticeable.

Interpreting Auras

Once you start to see auras, you can begin to interpret them by thinking about the quality of the colour you are seeing, rather than about the colour itself. Is it clear and bright, or dull and muddy? Is the aura healthy and happy, or are you getting mixed signals? With practise you may begin to link certain shades or colours with emotions.

We all interpret colour in different ways, but it helps to have a guide; the list of qualities, shown opposite, is a good starting point.

RED
Survival, strength, motivation, energy, power, anger, change

ORANGE
Vitality, sexuality, exercise, pleasure, creativity, warmth, passion

YELLOW
Inspiration, power of the mind, study, ideas, cheerfulness

GREEN
Nature, balance, harmony, calm, love, compassion

BLUE
Communication, healing, teaching ability, inspiration, creativity

INDIGO
Vision, intuition, psychic ability

VIOLET
Wisdom, enlightenment, spiritual growth

PINK
Love, warmth, tenderness, youthfulness, nurture, innocence

GOLD
Love, prosperity, brilliance, creativity

WHITE
Purity

BLACK
Depression, crisis, renewal

BROWN
Practical ability, down-to-earth qualities, solidity, devotion, friendliness

EXERCISE:

Refocusing Your Eyes

Developing auric sight is often simply a matter of learning how to refocus your eyes. This exercise will help you to do that. The soft light of evening is a good time to do this exercise.

1. Hold your hand about 45cm (18in) from your eyes. Look at it, noticing its shapes, lines and texture.
2. Notice the outline of your fingers and thumb as you gently make a fist and then release your hand again.
3. Shift your attention from your hand to something in the distance. Let your hand remain central, but look through it to your object. Practise shifting your vision back and forth a few times.
4. Notice how different your hand looks as you adjust your focus. Rest your eyes for a moment, then repeat the exercise, but this time leave your eyes focused on the distant object beyond your hand and notice what you see. You might glimpse a small movement of light or energy around your hand or a double-etched image.

Telepathy

Telepathy is the mind-to-mind communication of thoughts, feelings and ideas through psychic power. The following exercises will help you learn to send and receive information telepathically.

EXERCISE:
Target Practice

For this exercise, you will need a partner to work with you. If you keep practising this exercise, you will get a clearer sense of what you are best at: sending or receiving telepathic communication.

1. Select a part of your friend's body as a target. Close your eyes and focus intensely on it. Don't tell your friend what body part you have chosen.
2. Imagine tickling it or patting it for a few moments. Concentrate on feeling the sensation yourself before sending it to your partner.
3. When you have finished sending the information, open your eyes and ask your partner if they felt or thought anything.
4. Switch roles and let your partner target parts of your body in the same way.

EXERCISE:

Sharpening Your Telepathic Skills

For this exercise you need to agree on a time when you and a friend can meditate for ten minutes in different locations. You then use the first five minutes to send a message, and the other five minutes to receive, making sure that your times are synchronized so that one of you receives as the other sends.

1. Start with a few deep breaths and concentrate on sending a message to your friend. Think of the message in whatever way you wish, but stick to a single representation.
2. When the time is up, take a few more deep breaths and shift into receiving mode. Open your mind to the message your friend is sending.
3. When the exercise is finished, write down everything you can remember about the message you sent and what you think you received.
4. Compare your experiences. How often were you right? How often were you wrong? Don't be discouraged if the results are poor at first; most people improve with practice.

EXERCISE:

Sending Messages to Others

The previous exercises have involved short-distance telepathy, but believe it or not, long-distance telepathy can work too.

1. Choose someone to whom you'd like to send good thoughts, then find a quiet, comfortable spot and ask that your energy be sent.
2. Now bring that person to mind, and breathe deeply and slowly. As you inhale, see and feel healing light stream into you to heal and bless you. As you exhale, see that wonderful healing energy go from you to the other person to strengthen them.
3. Do this for a few moments. See and feel the other person becoming strong.
4. Offer thanks for the healing and then bring the focus and energy back to you, taking time to see yourself healed and strengthened by the process.

Scanning People

This sort of scanning is about seeing the energy and thoughts of others. It may not happen right away, but if you practise the techniques in this chapter every day, you will eventually get the hang of it.

EXERCISE:
Top to Toe

Scanning can tell you a lot about the people you meet.

1. When you are introduced to someone new take a moment to imagine that person in a ball of light or pure energy.
2. Now mentally scan that person from top to toe, then from toe to top, noticing any words, images, colours, thoughts or sensations in your body – anything at all (however crazy) that comes up. Remember not to stare; you don't need to look directly at a person to scan them.
3. If you can, write these first impressions down and save them. Once you have got to know the other person better, look back at your notes. Were you right? Did your impressions make sense?

EXERCISE:

Reading People

It's best to do this exercise initially with someone you know well. When you feel comfortable with it, you can use it with people you may not know as well.

1. Ask someone you know well to sit opposite you and be silent for five minutes. Hold their hand and close your eyes. Pay attention to your heart and stomach, noticing what sensations you feel.

2. Breathe deeply and begin to sense information about the other person. Look at their face and their body. Notice any colours that surround them. Take your time. Don't talk or ask any questions; just wait for sensations, thoughts or feelings to pass to you. When you are ready, open your eyes and share the information you have received. Deliver it as positively as you can.

3. If you have tapped into an area that the person does not feel comfortable discussing, leave it. Instead shift to other impressions you received.

4. Move away from the other person and imagine yourself harmlessly breathing out all the feelings that are not yours and that do not belong to you. You should also ground yourself (see page 36).

Working With Matter

In this chapter we explore how you can influence objects, places and situations with your thoughts.

Psychics believe that thoughts can travel outside the body and be absorbed by your environment, and this would indeed account for the sense of atmosphere that you may feel in certain places or situations. The exercises that follow are all designed to help your mind and body become more sensitive to your environment and the objects within it so that you can keep growing and attracting success your way.

Tune Into Touch

Every day of your life you exchange energy with the people you meet. Picking up and giving off energy is called imprinting. Here are some ways in which your inner guide can help you receive imprints.

Physical and Emotional Sensations

When you first pick up an object, pay attention to what you feel and where on your body you feel it. You may feel certain physical sensations, such as an itch, ache or tingle. By relaxing and paying close attention to what you feel, you start to connect with the energy imprints on the object.

Sometimes you may feel strong emotions within you as you receive impressions. Usually the emotion you pick up on is the one most recently or most often experienced by the wearer. Take note of how you are feeling as well as of what you are seeing in your mind's eye.

Visual Images

Sometimes your inner guide will help you see things associated with an object: images, colours, people and so on. The hard part isn't seeing the information; it is gaining an understanding of what that information means. If you feel confused, remember that your intuition will always try to use images or thoughts to which you can relate.

EXERCISE:

Energizing Your Hands

This exercise helps to awaken the sensitivities in your hands, making it easier to use them to feel subtle energies on objects, people and places.

1. Rub the palms of your hands together for about 30 seconds, then extend your hands in front of you, with the palms facing down and about 60cm (2ft) apart.

2. Move your hands towards each other, bringing them as close as you can without letting them touch.

3. Now draw your hands slowly back, until they are about 20cm (8in) apart. Repeat this in-and-out movement two or three times and, as you do so, pay attention to what you feel. You may sense pressure building between your hands, feel a tickling sensation or sense a warming up or cooling down between your hands.

Psychometry

Reading the energy imprints on things and places is called psychometry. It can be a useful way of picking up information about something or somewhere. Information held in objects can be good, bad or indifferent. For example, if you pick up a bride's wedding veil, you might feel the excitement of the day.

EXERCISE:

Sensing the Colour of a Card

In this exercise you are going to try and sense the colour of the suits without looking at the cards. Red cards have a different energy and feel to black cards.

1. Get a pack of playing cards, then energize your hands (see page 68).
2. Place one black card in front of you and turn it face up. Place your hands over it, close your eyes and pay attention to what you feel. Do the same with a red card.
3. Now spread out the whole pack face down and choose a card. Keep it face down and try to feel if it is black or red. Turn the card over and see if you were correct; repeat with another card. You will be surprised at how quickly you improve.

EXERCISE:
Guess What?

Here is an exercise you might like to try with other people.

1. Ask some of your friends to bring some small objects, then place them in envelopes so that you have no idea which object belongs to whom.
2. Now energize your hands (see page 68).
3. Choose an envelope and take the object out.
4. Close your eyes and relax. Try to attune yourself to the object in your hands by paying attention to any physical, emotional and visual sensations that come to you. Start with the physical sensations. Do you feel hot, cold, itchy? Does a part of your body tingle or appear before your mind? Next, concentrate on your emotions. Finally, concentrate on whatever images come to mind.
5. When you have finished sensing everything, write down all your impressions on the envelope and share your experience with the owner of the object. Get as much detail and feedback as you can, and don't worry if you get things wrong – it isn't a contest.

Sensing Atmospheres

Just as objects have their own energy and feel, so everything that happens in an object's environment affects it and can be registered by those with psychic – and in particular clairsentient – ability.

EXERCISE:

Sensing Places

In this exercise you will think about the places in your life where you spend a lot of time in order to help you observe your impressions of the world around you.

1. Write down the places where you spend most of your time.
2. Consider what places leave you with a good impression? What places leave you feeling unsettled? Think about which places are good for you and which aren't. You may discover that certain rooms in your house, or sections of a particular road, are not as good as others. You don't need to give a reason why, or look for any cause.
3. Once you have made your observations, you may want to talk to a friend about them. You may be surprised how often other people feel the same way, for no apparent reason.

EXERCISE:

Getting to Know a Room

This exercise is designed to help you detect feelings and atmospheres around you right now.

1. Walk around the room you are in, or go to another room in your house (not your bedroom).
2. How light or dark is it? What colours are in it? What shapes? How warm or cold is it? What sounds do you hear? What does it smell like?

3. Now put your hand on your stomach and notice how you feel about this room. Is the area relaxed or tense? Does the room have a personality? Is there a happy atmosphere? Are the people who use this room happy, or is there some stress? Has anything happened in the past in this room to influence the present?

4. Trust your gut instincts to give you the answers. If the room doesn't feel balanced, ask yourself what needs to change to improve the atmosphere so that your feelings might be better. You could do this by rearranging the furniture, hanging pictures on the walls or inviting more positive people and experiences into your room.

Telekinesis

Telekinesis is the ability to move objects using thoughts and energy alone. It is not an easy power to develop, and the great majority of people would benefit more from investing their energies in other areas of psychic development. Having said that, who knows what someone is capable of, given the right practice? It is vital to note that if you don't accept that you have the potential to harness the power of telekinesis, your mind will work against you.

EXERCISE:

Moving Small Items

The idea of being able to make large, heavy objects fly around the room is magical, but the reality is not quite so dramatic. Small, light objects, such as pieces of paper or pins, are far more likely to be moved using this skill, so try with these first.

1. Energize your hands according to the guidelines already given (see page 68).
2. Place them near a small object, such as a little piece of kitchen foil or a used match. Cup your hands around the item until you can sense the edge of its energy.
3. Once you can feel this, try to visualize the energy flowing from your hands into the item, and imagine moving it with this energy. Be patient, for it takes time to build and release the energy in the right way for the object to respond.
4. Practise for a few minutes every day. If you keep practising, in time the object may move or twitch – this is your telekinetic influence on it. Keep doing this exercise with different types of objects in different environments.

Working With Time

In this chapter we get to grips with psychic abilities that are "time-based" using divination tools such as scrying, Tarot cards and dreams. Whichever method you choose, it is important to understand that each time you reach out to your subconscious power, your connection to it will grow stronger and you will increase your psychic ability.

Keep in mind that you create possibilities in the future through choices and actions in the present. So, in many ways you can see into your future by recognizing the patterns of behaviour that set you up for success or failure. The key is to be able to recognize these patterns, and the best way to do that is to establish a strong connection with your intuition by working through the exercises in this book.

Scrying

Traditionally a crystal ball is used in scrying, but you don't have to use one. Some psychics can scry on any surface they choose, such as a mirror, a bowl of water or even their fingernails. However, when you begin scrying you may want to use a quartz crystal and/or a bowl of water.

EXERCISE:

Simple Scrying

With every attempt at scrying you strengthen your ability, and in time the images you see will become clearer.

1. Begin with slow, rhythmic breathing, and place your hands around a crystal or a bowl of water.

2. Focus on what the problem is or on what you want to know. As you hold or touch the crystal or bowl of water, feel it coming to life. Imagine that energy is growing within you.

3. Stay relaxed and pay attention to the formations you see in the crystal or bowl – watch how the light reflects or catches. Don't stare too hard; just look softly.

4. Your intuition will help you recognize images that relate to your question. Ask yourself what they mean to you. You will see clouds appearing and disappearing, and you may even catch glimpses of the future. Your state of mind when scrying will need to be calm and focused.

Tarot Cards

A Tarot deck consists of 78 cards divided into two groups: the major arcana (22 cards) and the minor arcana (56 cards). There are four suits in each deck: pentacles, swords, cups and wands. This may sound really complicated, but in essence the cards are simply triggers for your intuition.

Typically, Tarot cards are read by shuffling the deck and then laying out the cards, face down in various formations or spreads. Each position in the spread is thought to have a particular meaning and significance, and each major or minor arcana card laid down has an individual meaning.

Although spreads are most commonly used for divinatory purposes, results can also be achieved by analysing just one card picked at random. In fact, some people like to draw a single card at the start of each day and meditate on it, to trigger their intuitive powers.

EXERCISE:
The Touchstone Spread

This exercise is a great way to get to know the cards one at a time.

1. At the beginning of each day, spread out all the cards face down.
2. Then choose one at random, using it as a reference point for the events that lie ahead that day.
3. At the end of the day reflect on what has happened, and how the card you picked either summed up or provided a commentary on these events.

Dreams

Every time you go to sleep, you cross a mysterious threshold of consciousness. Dreams can help us make sense of what happened during the day, aid in solving problems, present opportunities to play out our desires, and confront our fears and use scenarios to communicate messages about our past, present and future.

A good way to uncover the meaning of your dreams is by free association: simply go with the first thing that pops into your mind. The more you work with your dreams, the more familiar you will become with your personal images. In the often surreal world of dreams there is no place for logic, and the answer to your question may feature in your dream even before the question has been raised.

EXERCISE:
Dream Incubation

This exercise will encourage your waking mind to work with your sleeping mind to help you solve problems in your waking life.

1. Decide what you want to dream about, what problem you want resolved or question you want answered. Write your question or desired dream on a piece of paper. Be as specific as you can.
2. Read this over and over again during the day, and again as you get ready for bed.
3. Once in bed, read the question again and ask your dreaming self to bring you the answer during sleep. Put the paper under your pillow or near your bed.
4. Tell yourself that you will have the dream you asked for, and trust that you will.
5. Tell yourself you will remember your dream. Be prepared to write it down when you wake up and be open to whatever comes to you.
6. Leave your dream intention to incubate. Relax your mind before you sleep. Be willing to experiment and try again if necessary.

Synchronicity

Have you ever found yourself in exactly the right place at the right time? Has the phone ever rung with an answer to a question exactly when you most needed it? Many people brush such common experiences aside as mere coincidences, but there is nothing insignificant about them. They are examples of synchronicity.

As you start to work with the exercises in this book, you will not only begin to hear your intuition; you will also start to recognize the signs of synchronicity.

Developing Synchronicity

Until you gain confidence in your ability to pick up the subtle clues of synchronicity, here are a few exercises to help you tune in.

- As you're waking up in the morning, see if you can get any impressions of the day's news headlines before you hear or read them.
- Before you turn on the radio, see if you can guess what music will be playing.
- Next time you are at a bank of lifts, see if you can guess which one is going to arrive next.
- When you are at the supermarket checkout, try to guess which queue is going to be fastest.

Working With Other Dimensions

In this chapter you will learn how to develop skills to see beyond physical barriers to other locations, and – for those who believe there is more to this life than merely material reality – how to experience other dimensions of existence.

We all have a higher self or consciousness that helps to guide the course of our lives. The higher self is a part of our mind that acts as a bridge between the physical and spiritual realms. Most people keep their higher self hidden away deep within themselves, but with every psychic-development exercise you have done so far in this book, and will do in this chapter, it is becoming stronger and more powerful in your daily life.

Remote Viewing

Remote viewing is the psychic ability to witness events, objects or locations beyond the range of the human eye. For example, a viewer might be asked to describe a location on the other side of the world, which they have never visited; an event that happened long ago; or an object sealed in a container or locked in a room – all without being told anything about the target (not even its name or designation).

EXERCISE:

Remote-Viewing Exercise

Try remote viewing for yourself with this simple exercise.

1. Choose a place that you wish to visit, but haven't yet been to, and about which you know very little. If you are with a friend, you could choose something like their office, or a relative's home.
2. After choosing your "target", get comfortable and close your eyes. Take several breaths and imagine you are floating gently out of your body and moving to the site you have chosen. Begin to notice and describe the details of what you see.
3. When you have seen enough, float back into your physical body and take some deep breaths. Do some stretching and give yourself a few moments to come back into the room.
4. Write down everything you can recall from your experience. Bear in mind that you may feel as if you are just making things up, but when you do eventually visit your chosen location, you may be surprised to find that you were more accurate than you thought you would be. Be willing to take a risk, even if it means being wrong.

EXERCISE:

Connect With Your Higher Awareness and Meet Yourself

The higher self is a part of our mind that acts as a bridge between the physical and spiritual realms. Getting in touch with your higher self may seem strange and awkward at first, but the more you practise it, the more you will be able to incorporate psychic abilities into your life.

This exercise will help you to meet your inner guide.

1. Sit comfortably, breathe deeply, close your eyes and imagine that your higher self exists in a beautiful place of light and sound, and that the place is right above you.

2. As you breathe, visualize a bridge leading to your higher self and see yourself climbing onto it. As you enter your higher self you are surrounded by light, colour and sound. Take the time to explore.
3. When you are ready, see in front of you a full-length mirror. You realize that the image you see in the mirror is the real you, the ideal you – your higher self. To your amazement, your higher self steps out of the mirror and says, "I am the most creative part of you. I see that which you do not. How can I help you?" The voice is kind, gentle and loving.
4. Sit down with your higher self and ask it what lies ahead for you in the coming week. Listen and remember what your higher self has to say. Your guide tells you that it is always with you, then melts into you so that you feel your true essence awakening.
5. Your heart is filled with hope. You are greater than you can imagine. As you leave, bring that feeling of inspiration with you to your daily life.
6. Walk back across the bridge and, as you do so, see yourself expressing your higher awareness in every waking moment.
7. Gradually open your eyes and make note of any insights that have come to you.

EXERCISE:

Working With Chakras: Third-Eye Meditation

You may already have come across the word chakra; it is a Sanskrit word that means "wheel". Chakras are the centres of energy activity in the body, handling all life energies for us. Information from your higher self can be received through all the chakras but the forehead centre (or third eye, as it is also known) is most commonly associated with the development of psychic, and in particular clairvoyant, potential.

Your third eye is a doorway to your higher self and unknown potential. This meditation will help you open that doorway.

1. Relax your mind and body, and breathe deeply. Inhale slowly and deeply through your nose, holding your breath for as long as is comfortable, before letting it out through the mouth. Repeat for four more breaths.

2. Focus your mind on the space in front of your forehead and imagine a movie screen there. Don't try to think about what is appearing on the screen; simply let images drift across it and focus on them as they come and go. Your third eye is opening.

3. Look for a colour on the movie screen and, when you see it, ask yourself what that colour could mean. Now look for shapes, and question yourself in the same way. As you do so, visualize yourself moving closer to the image until you can almost touch it. What do you see? What do you feel? Do you recognize it?

4. Now that your third eye is open, you can ask for a message. You need to be clear about what it is that you are asking for; you may want to write down a short sentence containing your question on a piece of paper.

5. Go through the process of relaxing and creating your movie screen. Watch the colours and shapes unfold and let the answer to your question reveal itself to you as words, images or colours on the screen. Just let the story unfold.

6. Record what you see. Does it make sense to you? Even if it doesn't make sense now, it might do so at some later date.

Also available